AF808668

# LASTING PROSPERITY

## Financial Wisdom from The Proverbs

Homes of Love

*For Scripture quotations all from the NKJV unless otherwise mentioned*
*New King James Version®. Copyright © 1982 by Thomas Nelson.*
*Used by permission. All rights reserved.*
*Holy Bible, New International Version®, NIV® Copyright © 1973, 1978, 1984, 2011 by Biblica, Inc.® Used by permission. All rights reserved worldwide.*

Copyright © 2015, Homes of Love, Kansas City, Missouri, USA
www.homes-of-love.com
Translated from French by Francis and Helen Delpuech
(helenead@aol.com)
All rights reserved. No part of this book can be reproduced, copied or distributed in printed or electronic form without authorization.
First English edition: August 2015
Printed in the United States of America
ISBN: 978-1-943202-00-3

# LASTING PROSPERITY

## Financial Wisdom from The Proverbs

**Pierre Bezençon**

To my wife Laurence

Proverbs 31:10-31

# TABLE OF CONTENTS

Introduction ........ 7

**Chapter 1: Four Foundations of Lasting Prosperity** ........ 11

Work ........ 12
Righteousness ........ 14
Blessing ........ 17
Generosity ........ 20

**Chapter 2: Four Devourers of Lasting Prosperity** ........ 23

Laziness ........ 24
Unrighteousness ........ 28
Standing Surety ........ 30
Greed ........ 32

**Chapter 3: Four Prosperity Optimizers** ........ 37

Wisdom ........ 38
Patience ........ 41
Means of Production ........ 44
Contentment ........ 47

**Chapter 4: Three Prosperity Minimizers** ........ 51

Debt ........ 52
Pleasures ........ 55
Prestige ........ 57

**Chapter 5: Rich for What?** ........ 59

Honoring God First ........ 60
Helping the Poor ........ 62

# INTRODUCTION

A young man on the threshold of adult life wonders: How will I make it financially?

What advice would you give him? Have you answered the question for yourself? Do you know how to reach the level[1] of lasting prosperity God has reserved for your life?

Many forms of financial success glitter brightly: a job that pays very well, a career as a star in sports or show business, investments with high returns, the possibility of winning the lottery, the creation of a successful startup, a genius invention with a patent, or other unique opportunities to grab… All of this, though, seems to be reserved for a very small number of people, an elite of privileged ones.

**Nobody can condemn you to stay poor**

Is there a sure path, valid for all, to reach prosperity? Yes, and it is the good news of this book, for yourself and for those to whom you give advice.

[1] God gives a different measure of prosperity to each one according to His sovereignty and the task He appoints. He gives to each one the ability to get out of poverty by following His principles. The goal is not to become a millionaire, but to reach the full potential of prosperity that God has appointed for us without comparing ourselves to others.

Many years ago, a loving father dug into the love and wisdom of the Eternal Father, so he could communicate the secrets of life to his son. As a father, he echoed the voice of the Heavenly Father and left a treasure to humanity: the book of Proverbs. Divine wisdom takes into account all the complexity and the contradictions of human reality and marks a sure path that we are invited to follow.

Lasting prosperity is not the fruit of luck. It is acquired neither by shortcuts nor by miracle formulas. Nobody can communicate to you an anointing to become rich and nobody can condemn you to stay poor. Prosperity is the result of invariable laws and eternal principles valid for everyone, just like the law of gravity.

*"There may be no poor among you; for the Lord will greatly bless you in the land which the Lord your God is giving you to possess as an inheritance only if you carefully obey the voice of the Lord your God, to observe with care all these commandments which I command you today."*

Deuteronomy 15:4-5

## Chapter 1

# FOUR FOUNDATIONS OF LASTING PROSPERITY

## WORK

*"In all labor there is profit, but idle chatter leads only to poverty."*
Proverbs 14:23

*"He who tills his land will have plenty of bread, but he who follows frivolity will have poverty enough!"*
Proverbs 28:19

God placed man in the Garden of Eden to cultivate it. Work was given before the Fall. Nothing has changed since; it has not become a curse. Work is part of man's life and it is the first foundation of abundance. Provision without labor is a harmful illusion. God does not want to feed man without him making any effort. He does not want to miraculously provide for a living on a constant basis. Certainly, God gave manna to His people in the desert and He multiplied the fish and loaves to unveil the identity of His Son. These actions, so crucial in the lives of the children of God, remain as exceptions. The rule is: without working, we are headed toward poverty and shortage. On the other hand, the one who tends to his field has plenty of bread.

**Work has not become a curse**

Pictures of an easy life without working are carefully maintained in the media, but they are only delusions. Those who can afford the luxury to live on a fortune accumulated by others are rare. At the other end of the scale of wealth, social help seems to break the vital link between work and food. These concepts, disconnected from reality, throw many into confusion and draw them into dead-end paths. With the coming collapse of the all-providing governments and the fall of stock markets, the wake-up call will be hard for many. Life without work is simply not part of God's plan and those who follow it will suffer the consequences.

Our society encourages a large part of the population to adopt a position of passivity. Some become spectators, consumers, recipients of state aid or fall prey to lifelong victim mentality. Anyone can temporarily adopt one of these roles at some point in their lives without any detrimental consequences. But when this passivity becomes a lifestyle, then, it is destructive.

However, lack of work does not always mean lack of occupation. It is possible to become busy and produce nothing: "...he who follows frivolity will have poverty enough!" Some people go from entertainment to entertainment; others spend their energy thinking of who they could become. Their days are filled with the pursuit of vain things that do not bear fruit. They may be caught in many activities, but they do not harness themselves to a work that satisfies them.

Some may say that they cannot find a job, implying that they are not involved in a gainful activity. However, work is not limited to being hired. "Tilling his land" does not necessarily mean owning land, but increasing one's gifts and abilities. It is possible to work for yourself by developing skills, services or new products. Making efforts to acquire or improve one's abilities prepares future income. When others see our know-how and appreciate its value, paid work becomes a reality, either as an employee or self-employed. *"Do you see a man who excels in his work? He will stand before kings."* (Prov. 22:29)

**Developing skills prepares future income**

## RIGHTEOUSNESS

*"A good man leaves an inheritance to his children's children, but the wealth of the sinner is stored up for the righteous. Much food is in the fallow ground of the poor, and for lack of justice there is waste."*

Proverbs 13:22-23

There is a law inscribed in creation: the work of the just and the unjust produces abundant food. However, preservation of wealth is tied to justice: *"A good man leaves an inheritance to his children's children, but the wealth of the sinner is stored up for the righteous."* The just enjoys lasting fruit. The fruit of his work is passed on to his grandchildren because God preserves it.

The Scriptures frequently talk about the prosperity of the wicked which is scandalous to the just. But it is always highlighted that this wealth is not long-term. You just have to wait. The test of time does not lie. Labor and maneuvers of a man may allow him to acquire possessions; but in the course of time, God redistributes them according to His righteousness. A good man leaves an inheritance to his children's children, but the sinner leaves an "inheritance" to the righteous appointed by God. The unjust accumulates resources without knowing it and unwillingly for the righteous.

Many governments try to give the goods of the rich people to the poor following a utopian desire for a more just society. God does not redistribute the wealth of the rich to the poor, He transfers the goods of sinners to the righteous. God is not trying to make the rich or the poor richer. He wants to give resources to the righteous so they can use their wealth righteously. God does not favor the poor or the rich. He gives favor to the righteous, whatever the measure of their wealth. He opposes the unjust no matter the position they hold on the social scale. The Marxist view of class war does not reflect God's intention. The rich are not necessarily the "unjust" neither are the poor "just." Conversely, a capitalist interpretation could present the picture that opulence would become a manifestation of righteousness and lack evidence of wickedness. This last concept does not reflect divine perspective. Poverty or provision do not define man's righteousness. These categories are not superimposed.

**God does not favor the poor or the rich, He gives favor to the righteous**

*"Much food is in the fallow ground of the poor, and for lack of justice there is waste."* The work of the poor will promote him to a position of abundance, according to the laws that God has placed in creation. But this economic change does not say anything about his character. Work allows one to get out of poverty and to find abundance; righteousness allows one to keep it.

Men naturally seek after wealth. God seeks after righteousness. Many people are lured into quick gain and immediate prosperity, sometimes with no regard for equity. The shortcut of dishonesty or compromise is not the path on which the Scripture leads us. Righteousness is an essential dimension of God's path. Wealth without righteousness does not carry God's approval.

*"A good man leaves an inheritance to his children's children."* His inheritance is much more than his fortune. This man passes on his

goodness, his righteousness, his love for God and his perception of hard work to his descendants. He also leaves them his material riches. But these do not make sense outside of the context of his spiritual treasures. God first wants His children to be "rich in righteousness" before being "rich in money." His desire is for the whole inheritance to be passed onto the children's children. The inheritance is not limited to the handing down of material wealth. God aims to communicate the blessing from generation to generation, which includes the lessons of wisdom and righteousness with the prosperity that goes along with them.

**Work gives abundance, righteousness allows one to keep it**

## BLESSING

*"The blessing of the Lord makes one rich, and He adds no sorrow with it."*

Proverbs 10:22

Work provides abundant food. Righteousness helps to progressively transform provision into prosperity because God enables the retention of what has been acquired. The blessing brings still another dimension: *"The blessing of the Lord makes one rich."*

Certainly, not all wealthy people are blessed, since *"the wealth of the sinner is stored up for the righteous."* But it is certain that if a hard-working and righteous man becomes rich, the blessing of God is at work. His blessing rests on a righteous person and manifests itself in his activity. God blessed Isaac and he reaped a hundred times more seed than he had sown. The blessing of God provides multiplication to the work of a righteous man. Investors look for the most beneficial investments. The returns are measured in percentage. The yield is a fraction of what has been invested. For example, an excellent 15% rate will produce 1.15 to 1 after a year. As a point of comparison, Isaac received 100 to 1.

**The blessing of God provides multiplication to the work of the righteous man**

In the world of international finances, people who become very rich rapidly have experienced a multiplying factor of their assets. This type of phenomenon can be observed particularly with starting innovative companies that are evaluated in the stock market at 10, 100 or even 1,000 times their initial value. Globalization of the markets and new information technology allow this spectacular multiplication which is not necessarily tied to divine blessing.

God was with Joseph in Potiphar's house and made everything that he put his hand to successful. Blessing brings in a dimension of increase, success and achievement. It is the Lord's work on man's work. In other words, God joins His work to man's work. He accomplishes what man cannot realize, but He does not do what man can do. The blessing cannot be manifested in the life of one who does not undertake anything. There has to be groundwork that God is going to multiply or make successful.

**God joins His work to man's work**

God does not show partiality nor is He a respecter of persons. He commands the blessing on the basis of precise criteria known in the Scriptures. There are no secrets or mysteries. Anyone can access the information on the subject found in the Bible. There is no luck, nor chance, nor privileges. The laws of blessing do not change. The man who walks according to the righteousness that God demands is blessed.

In the biblical account which occurred in an agricultural society, the divine blessing was often manifested in extraordinary harvests or multiplication of livestock. Joseph and Daniel experienced several promotions to high ranks of political authority in foreign kingdoms. David experienced constant military success. Ezra and Nehemiah obtained specific favor which allowed them to participate in the rebuilding of Jerusalem. The blessing is manifested by the gift of supernatural success in what is undertaken, no matter the domain. It rests upon the man who pleases God and it is a sign of His approval.

## GENEROSITY

*"There is one who scatters, yet increases more; and there is one who withholds more than is right, but it leads to poverty. The generous soul will be made rich, and he who waters will also be watered himself."*

Proverbs 11:24-25

According to simple mathematics, the one who gives generously should have less. However, in the dynamics of divine finances, the opposite happens. God rewards generosity. He approves the one who gives with joy and He makes it known by watering the one who has been watering. A generous person is tuned in with God because liberality is His nature. God rejoices in giving. God loves to be generous and He is glad to see His children looking like Him.

Man without God considers that resources are limited and thinks in a closed circle. He believes that what comes out of his pocket will no longer be available. This is precisely thinking without God. The means of God are limitless. He raises and moves resources the way He wants and where He wants. He creates manna that did not exist and moves quails to the middle of the desert. These visible signs, which are exceptional in the history of the children of Israel, show how God works.

God rewards the generous man in multiple ways. He can give him new ideas, revolutionary inventions, innovative concepts, new manufacturing procedures or wise counsel. He can grant him faithful and able co-workers or make known his activity far away and, as a result, enlarge his customer circle. He helps him avoid taking ruinous paths or entering into costly legal suits. He can give him a promotion in his company or allow him to go work for another company that will compensate him more for his skills. God's means are unlimited and He is never short of ideas or solutions.

Generosity is important to God because it puts love above the search for gain. The Lord finds plenty of people who only think of becoming rich and are ready to trample on anyone to climb higher. When He sees someone who favors righteousness and compassion, He rejoices and wants to make him know His approval. He is going to enlarge his sphere of influence.

**Generosity is important to God because it puts love above the search for gain**

God loves the one who gives generously because it shows that riches are not his goal and that the love of money does not rule in his heart, but instead he has compassion for his neighbor. The Lord does not want prosperity to become an objective in itself. In divine thinking, wealth is a "by-product" of an existence lived according to God. It is a logical consequence of a life of work, righteousness and blessing, but it is never the targeted goal. God requires man to do what is good and not to accumulate possessions. The prosperity that He gives is a means to continue to love others on a larger scale. In the world, wealth means influence. By providing greater financial resources, God grants a larger impact to spread love and righteousness. Egotistical prosperity is nonsense in His eyes.

**Wealth is a "by-product", it is never the targeted goal**

When God finds a man who does not misappropriate for his own profit the wealth that He entrusts him with for others, He keeps on watering him. The thought that our money belongs to us reflects one of the lies about finances that is most deeply rooted in the human soul. Our life does not belong to us, much less our money. Our existence is God's as well as our riches. Everything is lent to us and He remains the owner. We will have to give account for the way we stewarded what was entrusted to us. Becoming rich leads to greater responsibility. Already prosperous, the man *"who scatters, yet increases more."* It is a paradox that generosity consolidates wealth.

## Chapter 2

# FOUR DEVOURERS OF LASTING PROSPERITY

## LAZINESS

*"Go to the ant, you sluggard! Consider her ways and be wise, which, having no captain, overseer or ruler, provides her supplies in the summer, and gathers her food in the harvest. How long will you slumber, O sluggard? When will you rise from your sleep? A little sleep, a little slumber, a little folding of the hands to sleep—so shall your poverty come on you like a prowler, and your need like an armed man."*

Proverbs 6:6-11

As surely as work leads to satisfaction, laziness brings shortage. Harvest rewards the one who tilled and sowed earlier during the year. The fruit of activity is often a long time coming. In the same way, the result of laziness does not come immediately. A person who gives himself to laziness does not bear the consequences instantly, but eventually he will feel the effects.

The ant prepares her food in summer and gathers her food during harvest. The lazy lets this season pass. He tries to escape the hard labor that defines it. He is reluctant to accumulate long hours of laborious work. He rests when the harvesters carry out their task. He enjoys himself when others labor and sweat. He does not participate in the general effort.

**Poverty will visit lazy people**

Poverty will visit lazy people like a prowler. The time is not precisely set, but it will come. Like a thief that steals goods to fill his stomach in his wanderings, poverty comes first to take away goods from the house of the lazy. It is a first warning signal. But one day, shortage comes in like an armed man; it besieges him and does not leave him until it overcomes him. Poverty comes forcefully, it comes armed, and it imposes itself on him. It settles and the lazy cannot get rid of it anymore.

A lazy person lives for the moment. He does not think of the future. He wants to take advantage of the present time. His life is stamped by his feelings and immediate emotions. He does what pleases him in the moment. When it is the season to harvest and participate in hard labor under a scorching sun, a lazy man is nowhere to be found. When the time comes to plow, he thinks that the conditions are too painful for him. The cold and the hard work of tilling the land easily put him off. *"The lazy man will not plow because of winter; he will beg during harvest and have nothing*[2]*."* A lazy person refuses to make any effort in difficult conditions. He is led by circumstances; he always looks for the easy path, he does not have any perseverance or endurance. At harvest time, he would like to reap, but there is nothing for him. He wishes to participate in the benefits without contributing to the work they require. His search for an easy life will lead him, one day or another, to lacking the basic necessities of life. Today, many lazy people gather together under the banner of a "relaxed" lifestyle and a "cool" identity. Their creed is "stay cool", "enjoy" and "have fun". They usually share the opinion that those who work hard are doing too much. The terminology has changed, but the reality has stayed the same.

**A lazy man wishes to participate in the benefits without contributing to the work they require**

[2] Proverbs 20:4

God wants man to work on earth for many reasons. His desire for him is to participate in His creative work. He gives him a place to exercise his freedom and his authority. He delights his heart with the fruit of his work. He puts in front of him challenges that will cause him to grow and search for His counsel. Through work He structures his daily, weekly and yearly life. God provides him with an occupation and a rhythm that protects him from many drifts of idleness. He teaches him to learn how to collaborate with other people and allows exchanges that would never take place otherwise, so that he develops respect for the skills of others. There are still many more reasons for which God assigns work to man but one aspect is worth underlining: work keeps man humble.

**Work keeps man humble**

A person who is not confronted with the daily difficulties of labor might lose the right measure of himself. The obstacles, challenges, setbacks, confrontations, limitations and failures linked to his activity help him to keep a humble attitude. A man who works knows that he is not all-powerful. He is aware of the fact that he does not have all the solutions. Through experience, he realizes that he needs to continue to learn. He sees that he needs God and others. A lazy person runs the risk of falling into the trap of pride and contempt of others. *"The lazy man is wiser in his own eyes than seven men who can answer sensibly*[3]*."*

Laziness generates a feeling of superiority. A lazy man puts himself above the rules. He does not need to make any effort while everybody else is working hard, harvesting or

[3] Proverbs 26:16

tilling the land. He does not see why he should wear himself out and thinks that workers do not understand how to enjoy life. As long as his entourage, his company or social welfare provide for him, he thinks he is shrewder than anyone else. He even goes to the point of despising the government, tax-payers or his relatives who feed him. As long as the system works without a real effort on his part, a lazy man thinks that he is wise and he does not listen. It is not possible to reason with him. Only shortage will bring him back to his senses.

*"The lazy man says, 'There is a lion outside! I shall be slain in the streets!*[4]*"* He finds frivolous excuses for not working. He lives outside of reality. He deceives himself and imagines he is fooling others. His reasoning is corrupted and leads to absurd conclusions. But he still believes them, even if he is the only one. A lazy man always has objections when it is time to make an effort.

Such a person can hide behind a paid job. He is not necessarily on welfare, because laziness is an attitude that takes many forms. Lazy men search for loopholes in the system where little effort is required, either in public service or in companies. Their internal disposition shows its real face when there is no manager, supervisor or anyone else to control productivity. God is not fooled, and one day or another, for example in circumstances like a restructuring, a mass lay-off, or an economic crisis, shortage lays siege to a lazy person like an armed man.

[4] Proverbs 22:13

## UNRIGHTEOUSNESS

*"There is desirable treasure, and oil in the dwelling of the wise, but a foolish man squanders it."*

Proverbs 21:20

In Proverbs, "the wise" refers to the man who lives according to God's wisdom. He has learned the righteous ways of the Creator, and applies them in his practical life. "The fool" does not describe the man who has a low I.Q., but someone who does not want to learn what God is teaching. The fool is characterized by ungodliness. He opposes himself to the divine wisdom and lives against God's laws. If the wise is the model and the hero of Proverbs, the fool is the counter-model and the anti-hero.

A righteous man (the wise) ends up accumulating precious treasures in his house. His life of work and righteousness combined with the blessing of God have provided him with prosperity. The fool can also have acquired riches by his labor or by unrighteous means. However, his opulence will be swallowed up by his lack of righteousness. His ungodly, foolish behavior will diminish his wealth. His life choices, that are not inspired by God's wisdom, will devour the measure of prosperity he has acquired.

A typical example is given to us in the area of morality *"...But a companion of harlots wastes his wealth*[5]*."* When behaviors divert from God's will, there is a negative effect in the financial area. Sin is costly. In absolute terms, concerning our positioning before God, sin is certainly costly, but this reality affects also the finances. Prostitution,

[5] Proverbs 29:3

gambling, excessive drinking, drugs, witchcraft, extortion or other transgressions can literally ruin a family.

The ways of the Lord preserve our happiness within different spheres of our existence. When one deviates from them, it brings along all kinds of tragedy: personally, in the family, at work and in the social sphere, as well as in the financial one. God knows that finances touch the heart of a man and He uses them to call him back to Himself. The effects on finances constitute a visible reality signaling that something is wrong and must be corrected. Whatever their grandeur and their well-established position, colossal fortunes and financial empires have been swallowed up by sinful behavior. When this downward spiral is set in motion, it is really time to come back to God and to His will.

**Colossal fortunes and financial empires have been swallowed up by sinful behavior**

## STANDING SURETY

*"Do not be one of those who shakes hands in a pledge, one of those who is surety for debts; if you have nothing with which to pay, why should he take away your bed from under you?"*

Proverbs 22:26-27

Standing surety is a trap, even if it comes from noble feelings. When a member of the family or a dear friend needs to take out a loan, one must not sign for him. It is not the right solution.

Committing to someone else's debt can lead to your own ruin. The warning is strong and without question: standing surety must be avoided at all cost. In fact, it is based on several dysfunctions. It is wrong to commit to it for three main reasons:

First, the responsibility of the loan does not rest on its beneficiary. This situation deprives the one who wants to go into debt of his responsibility and places the burden of what is owed on the one who has signed the guarantee. It is always easier to borrow if ultimately, someone else will have to assume the repayment. So, the one who has stood surety is at the mercy of the one he wanted to help. He will have to suffer the consequences of the decisions and behavior of someone other than himself. He has lost control of the situation.

**The one who has stood surety is at the mercy of the one he wanted to help**

Secondly, standing surety is wrong because it allows a person to get into debt that would otherwise be impossible to incur. A bank that refuses a loan to someone without someone else's signature, surely has its reasons: the financial situation of the person will probably not allow him to honor his commitments. It is a warning that must be taken into account. One must have the courage to tell the person who wants to borrow that he is not in a position to do so.

**One must have the courage to tell the person who wants to borrow that he is not in a position to do so**

Thirdly, the one who is standing surety probably does not have the means to reimburse what he is signing for. If he had this money available, he could himself take the role of the bank and lend it to his friend or his family under certain conditions. Affectionate feelings or clever emotional manipulation can lead him to go beyond reasonable limits, but pride can also push him forward. Actually, vanity can be flattered by the idea of helping someone, even if it is a delusion. Later, the awakening will be harsh when the bailiff will take even the bed on which he was resting.

In His goodness, God certainly wants to spare us useless suffering.

## GREED

*"A man with an evil eye hastens after riches, and does not consider that poverty will come upon him."*

Proverbs 28:22

Prosperity comes as the result of a life of work and righteousness. It is given moreover, as a crown. To stay healthy it must not become a goal. When it becomes an objective to hit, it becomes toxic. It produces the opposite result of what was sought after. It carries in itself the seed of its own destruction. The greedy man who desires to become rich quickly thinks that he will achieve abundance. In reality, greediness sets off a process of long-term poverty. Covetousness can produce a few immediate results, but the gain does not last over time. The practice of industrial fishing which puts in danger even the survival of the fish, illustrates it. Cupidity leads to the plundering of human and natural resources without having any long-term perspective. A society hungry for short-term profits prepares a global economic crisis (a shortage). The search for immediate benefits kills the planning of long-lasting projects and endangers the next generation. The common sense investments necessary to prepare for the distant future are systematically put aside.

**Greed sets off a process of long-term poverty**

A greedy man becomes hard in business, but overall he becomes hard at heart. Sometimes caricaturists draw those who are desperate for gain as sharks. Greed distorts the relationship with God, with others, with money and with work. Prosperity becomes an idol to which one sacrifices a lot of things, particularly the sense of justice, family life, the respect of others and even sometimes one's health. The person who lets greed dwell in him becomes imperceptibly insensitive to God and others. Hardness takes the place of compassion. Money becomes more important than people, even the closest ones. *"He who is greedy for gain troubles his own house...*[6]*"*

With greed, work changes its status. Gain becomes its driving force. Activity is only a means to "make money." It is no longer about serving others with the gifts God has entrusted to us. Everyone is put under pressure to produce and bring back more. Greediness changes the rhythm of production and the quality of life at work. A profit must be made quickly and employees are squeezed like lemons in order to draw the maximum out of them. Choices are made according to the law of short-term productivity, regardless of other considerations of wisdom and justice. Everything available must be gathered rapidly even if the reserves become drained. A man with an evil eye hastens after riches, and does not consider that poverty will come upon him. Covetousness blinds him; it twists his judgment. Decisions made under its influence are not wise in the long-term and will destroy even the foundations of lasting prosperity. For example, over-intensive usage of farming land brings depletion of the soil.

[6] Proverbs 15:27

Envy never says "it is enough." It always generates dissatisfaction. It drives to get even more. It wants a growth and an increase in profits. Greed pushes man forward and drags him on a foolish race. It pulls him out of God's rhythm which is characterized by peace and trust. In this stress, man loses vision of the essential and does not make decisions that are beneficial to his future and to those surround him. That is why God opposes greediness[7] and His judgment is sooner or later manifested in the natural. Greediness leads to a dead end. The one who follows it commits himself to a dead end road. He will have to make a u-turn. He is searching for riches, but he will encounter poverty, first for his own soul and then for his pocket-book.

[7] Proverbs 1:19 ; Proverbs 10:3

## *SYNTHESIS: REMAIN ON THE FOUNDATIONS AND KEEP THE DEVOURERS AWAY UNTIL THE END*

In the first chapter, we established the following equation:

Work + righteousness + blessing + generosity = lasting prosperity

In the second chapter, we established the following equation:

Laziness, unrighteousness, standing surety and greed (alone or together) will devour prosperity and lead to poverty.

It is essential to understand that the four foundations of lasting prosperity must be kept until the end of the road. The upward spiral of abundance never stops as long as these four values remain. So, it is important to continue our activity when we have reached wealth and not to give into the temptation of laziness. Too many wealthy people enter into idleness thinking wrongly that they do not need to work anymore. They do not see the need to earn their bread because they have all they desire[8]. They are reluctant to make any effort and become lazy. The downward spiral is underway for them and their riches will start diminishing. In the same way, many who have become opulent, start to compromise with

> **Too many wealthy people enter into idleness**

[8] *"The person who labors, labors for himself, for his hungry mouth drives him on."* Proverbs 16:26

righteousness. Their riches give them the illusion that they are above the law because some people bow before them and flatter them. They think they are protected by their prosperity[9]. They forget that God makes His blessing rest only on the righteous.

New temptations come up on this path to riches. The prosperous man encounters situations that are unknown to poor people and to those who only have the bare essentials of life. He faces the seduction of riches with a new intensity. Continuous purity of heart is not given to him at the beginning of his journey. He is going to face the same temptations of laziness, unrighteousness, pride and greediness as all wealthy people before him. Statistics show that, in a general sense, the more riches increase, the more generosity diminishes. So, staying generous when we possess a lot is a very real fight.

## *REFLECTIONS*

- What are the foundations of lasting prosperity that are already in place in my life?

- Have I noticed that some foundations are more established than others? If yes, which ones would need some solidifying?

- Have I noticed the presence of prosperity devourers in my life? Which ones? What do I need to do in order to get rid of them?

- Have I reached a level of prosperity that exposes me to new temptations (laziness, unrighteousness, standing surety or greediness) that I had overcome in the past? How can I come back to the foundations?

[9] *"The rich man's wealth is his strong city, and like a high wall in his own esteem."* Proverbs 18:11

## Chapter 3

# FOUR PROSPERITY OPTIMIZERS

## WISDOM

*Wisdom declares: "Riches and honor are with me, enduring riches and righteousness. My fruit is better than gold, yes, than fine gold, and my revenue than choice silver. I traverse the way of righteousness, in the midst of the paths of justice, that I may cause those who love me to inherit wealth, that I may fill their treasuries."*

Proverbs 8:18-21

Wisdom is characterized neither by accumulation of knowledge nor by uncommon intelligence. The wise is someone humble who wants to be taught by God. He wishes to know the ways of the Creator. He desires to understand the manual of life. He is searching for his bearings in the labyrinth of contradictions and the mysteries of existence. He attempts to pierce through the laws that rule human relationships. He aims to find the constants that usher into happiness and the invariables that lead to sorrow. To do so, he positions himself to listen to his Creator and prays: "Teach me."

**The wise desires to know the ways of the Creator**

The first lesson of wisdom is the fear of the Lord, which will direct a man's whole existence toward righteousness (and not toward gain). Divine wisdom and love for righteousness are deeply connected. God loves righteousness and He appreciates a person who lives according to it. Wisdom consists in being of one mind with the Creator and of cherishing righteousness equally. Like the mechanism of a clock of great precision, where each part hinges in detailed complexity, righteousness allows the wheels of life to adjust harmoniously. It makes married life, friendship and business a success, and leads to prosperity. On the other hand, unrighteousness, like a particle of sand, jams and sometimes completely stops this very delicate mechanism. Divine wisdom positions us in a right relationship with the essential realities of our existence. This way, we learn to have the right attitude towards God, our parents, our spouse, our children, our body, our authorities, the wicked, the wise, our job and our money.

**Righteousness allows the wheels of life to adjust harmoniously**

Divine wisdom transmits to us the keys of happiness on earth. It shows us the path to obtaining the profound desires of our being. However, this path is often paradoxical and a detour is necessary to reach the goal. So, in the area of finances, chasing after riches prevents us from becoming prosperous. On the other hand, acquiring wisdom opens the way to prosperity. In fact, it fills up the treasuries of those who love it. Wealth is a logical consequence of it. So, how do we orient ourselves in this labyrinth? How can a man know that the direct path does not reach the goal? How can he understand that he needs to choose another direction to finally arrive at his destination? The instruction of God is necessary to lead a man to the goal.

**Wisdom will produce prosperity**

The fruit of wisdom is better than gold. Wisdom will produce prosperity, but it will bear a fruit that is better than abundance alone. It will give wealth with an atmosphere of righteousness and peace. This way, financial success loses its toxic character because it is placed in a new frame of understanding. It is no longer oriented toward egotistical goals, but it is submitted to God's objectives, particularly righteousness and mercy. When wisdom comes first, man is freed of the obsession of becoming rich. He knows the satisfaction of being in harmony with his Creator and that gives him contentment regardless of what he does or does not possess. Certainly, goods make life more pleasant and comfortable, but they are no longer at the center of his preoccupations and his decisions.

> **With righteousness and peace, financial success loses its toxic character**

The acquisition of wisdom is neither a loss of time nor a loss of money. On the contrary, it is an investment that will produce big returns in the long run. *"Wisdom is the principal thing; therefore get wisdom. And in all your getting, get understanding."* (Proverbs 4:7). Only a small number of people realize the importance of knowing God's ways and decide to enroll in His divine wisdom school. Investing many hours and several years, as well as significant financial resources, to study the Scriptures is a wise decision. Unfortunately, many think that it is more important to invest time and money to acquire technical or linguistic competence in order to "succeed in life."

# PATIENCE

*"Dishonest money dwindles away, but whoever gathers money little by little makes it grow."*

Proverbs 13:11(NIV)

Riches that increase little by little are a blessing. It is neither an anomaly, nor a failure, nor a problem. It is the model God has in store for those whom He loves.

The media likes to speak of people who increase their possessions suddenly and spectacularly. The possibility of acquiring a fortune from one day to another is a persistent and harmful illusion. The idea that all it takes is a strike of the magic wand of destiny and a lot of luck to bring it to pass, feeds the dream of millions of people. These are all just lies and mystification. Statistics show that 98% of lottery winners are poorer five years later than before winning the jackpot.

Lasting prosperity comes little by little. To be established, an increase of possessions must be slow and progressive. Management and preservation of wealth must be learned. The one who receives a fortune suddenly or increases his possessions rapidly does not have the experience and most of all the character training it requires. Young people who use their first salary well are often those who have learned to manage their allowance well and what they have earned with little jobs. Having goods requires making decisions that will result in squandering, conserving or increasing one's possessions.

**Lasting prosperity comes little by little**

Prosperity includes a few rules. There is a financial and economical know-how that is transmitted from generation to generation. It is encouraging to see that the lessons of wisdom learned by the parents are generally passed on to the children. But it is equally afflicting to see that all a generation has not learned is also transmitted to the following one. If work, righteousness and generosity are communicated to the descendants, so are endemic laziness, dishonesty and avarice. Nevertheless, each one can learn by listening to the divine wisdom no matter what his family environment was and in this way acquire the rules and character that invariably bring prosperity for several generations.

**There is a financial and economical know-how that is transmitted from generation to generation, nevertheless each one can learn by listening to the divine wisdom**

*"Whoever gathers money little by little makes it grow."* The man who is able to generate a surplus and save it, step-by-step, positions himself to become prosperous. In some countries, banks understand this principle. They only give a mortgage to those who have saved a minimum of 20% out of their own funds. The one who is able to consistently put money aside has already acquired several economic lessons, which shows that he will be able to reimburse his loan. When the government reduces the personal fund portion in order to help the unprivileged access property, it ends up in failure. On a national level, experience shows that most of those who have been assisted in such a way were not successful in keeping their house, after only a few years.

The man who gathers little by little increases his riches. His savings show that he is not spending all that he possesses. On one hand, he is able to restrain himself because he is pursuing an objective and on the other hand, he knows that increasing his goods is neither easy nor fast and that he has to make a long-term effort. His savings are probably the product of many hours of overtime work and the renunciation of much leisure. He knows the value of what he has. He will do all he can to preserve it. The one who acquires a fortune without any effort does not maintain the same relationship with money. He can cheaply sell off his possessions at the first opportunity without too much thought, because he did not sweat to obtain what he possesses.

Wisdom allows one to understand that the model of God concerning prosperity is a progressive increase of riches. This reality removes a lot of pressure and frees us up. It is useless and unnecessary to hurry. Riches, according to God, come like a ripe fruit in its season, before that it is green and sour. Time is an essential element. Wisdom teaches us to walk at God's pace. Wanting to arrive ahead of Him and make a fortune for ourselves without taking into account His timing is counter-productive. God's wisdom allows us to live with a peace that those who run after riches do not know. We avoid the stress and the pitfalls of those who want to go faster than God. Trust and patience protect us. We have no need to take inconsiderate risks searching for a quicker gain or juicier returns.

**The model of God, concerning prosperity is a progressive increase of riches**

## MEANS OF PRODUCTION

*"Where no oxen are, the trough is clean; but much increase comes by the strength of an ox."*

Proverbs 14:4

The use of the strength of animals or machines multiplies the product of human work. Good tools increase productivity and allow the generating of new income. So, it is important to invest in the means of production that increase the work efficiency of man. Using the biblical example, plowing with the help of oxen allows one to work many fields instead of only one, and in so doing, to put more crops in the barn. In the same way, felling trees with a chain-saw allows one to cut down many more trees than with a hand-saw. Doing office work with computers requires less time and allows one to process more data than without this tool.

**Means of production increase the work efficiency of man**

Before engaging in an expense, it is important to differentiate what is a means of production from what is not. A vacuum cleaner used in a home makes work easier, but it is not a tool of production. It enables the removal of dust week after week rapidly and easily but it does not generate income. On the other hand, an industrial vacuum cleaner in a cleaning company becomes a means of production that allows the improvement of productivity and consequently of income. Also, a truck can be used for leisure or as a means of production. It can be bought just for the fun of driving it. On the other hand, an independent contractor can use a truck to carry loads of construction materials and tools. In summary the means of production makes it possible to do a larger amount of work with more efficiency.

As soon as our prosperity allows it, it is important to use part of our goods to acquire some means of production. These investments will generate new income. Not all we have available should be spent to increase our comfort or our pleasure. Wealth belongs to those who have the means of production. God blessed Joseph in Potiphar's house, but Joseph could not reap the material benefits because he owned nothing and did not have any means of production. Potiphar had elevated him in dignity and authority, but he kept the profits of the work accomplished and of the blessing that rested upon Joseph.

**God blessed Joseph, but Joseph could not reap the material benefits because he owned nothing and did not have any means of production**

The means of production in which we need to invest must relate to our activity and allow us to become more efficient. It allows us to keep the fruit of our work without others taking possession of it. Farmers who do not have the means to preserve or package their merchandise are forced to abandon their crop at very low prices to large distribution companies. Authors who do not have their own publishing company have no other choice than to accept the terms of the publishers.

It is not possible to acquire everything at once, but it is necessary to make investments (and choices) that position us more and more as producers and owners. It is important to progressively move away from a status of user, consumer and renter. One must have the courage to make the changes of equipment, knowledge or competencies that will allow us to be more efficient and keep our income.

**It is necessary to make choices that position us more and more as producers and owners**

The statement that the strength of an ox gives abundance is full of wisdom. Good practical common sense and concrete observations help us to lead a company toward success. Investments must be geared first toward simple and humble solutions that have proven themselves and improve productivity in a concrete way. It is not necessary to go fast. Taking time to reflect after gathering information is part of wisdom.

## CONTENTMENT

*"Better is a little with the fear of the LORD, than great treasure with trouble. Better is a dinner of herbs where love is, than a fatted calf with hatred."*

Proverbs 15:16-17

The real satisfactions of life are relational. Love fills the heart in a way that can never be equaled by goods. The presence of God fulfills man like no other reality. All material riches are incapable of bringing happiness in an environment of conflict and hatred. Many dramas are hidden behind the façade of magnificent mansions. Greed and avarice sow trouble[10].

The book of Proverbs does not speak highly of poverty. But if a choice has to be made between love with poverty and possessions with hatred, love always comes first. Without it the fatted calf is nothing. Without peace at home great treasures have no value. The plan of God for the wise man consists in experiencing good relationships and having possessions. Too many people sacrifice the love and peace of their home to accumulate more goods. Too many human beings watch more over the condition of their bank account than over the condition of their heart. When time comes to decide the great choices of life, one has to remember that love is always the priority. When we weigh the pros and cons to main making a good decision, we have to know that on the scale of God

**Love always weighs more on the scale of God**

[10] Proverbs 15:27

love always weighs more. Possessions, as appealing as they can be, are no match for it.

Contentment is an internal wealth that is not well-known. A person who is satisfied with what he possesses experiences great peace. His decisions are not motivated by dissatisfaction and frustration. A man who can say that what he has is sufficient for him, is much less vulnerable to compromise. Contentment gives him great strength that allows him to stay in righteousness and to continue to put love above his possessions. He can assert peacefully that a menu of herbs and love is better than a meal of meat and hatred.

**Contentment gives great strength**

Contentment must not be confused with resignation or passivity. The one who is happy with his present condition does not close the door to the possibility of improvement of his material condition in the future. He only wants to get to it in God's timing and with His means. He hopes without impatience, without resentment and without anguish. He desires to change his situation but not "at any cost." For him harmony with God and his family is non-negotiable.

In some countries it is common to think that both spouses must work full-time to feed their family. But sometimes they do not consider any other solution because they want to maintain a high level of life. Financial resources certainly allow them to maintain some status, but the accumulation of stress and tiredness has to be evaluated in the family equation, especially if it generates conflicts. Husband and wife need time and peace to grow their love and their understanding of each other. Of course, everyone hopes to have everything: double income and perfect love. But often, the dream does not match reality and a choice has to be made. At this point, wisdom reminds us: better to eat more vegetables and have more love than to eat more meat and have troubles. In the same way, it is certainly better to renounce the income of being paid double for overtime than to sacrifice the day consecrated to the Lord and to family relationships.

## *SYNTHESIS: THE FOUR PROSPERITY OPTIMIZERS*

Wisdom, patience, means of production and contentment allow optimization of the development of one's prosperity.

## *REFLECTIONS*

- What are the optimizers that have already allowed me to improve the development of my prosperity?
- What are the ones I still need to develop? And what is my strategy to do it?

## Chapter 4

# THREE PROSPERITY MINIMIZERS

## DEBT

*"The rich rules over the poor, and the borrower is servant to the lender."*

Proverbs 22:7

Loans are not entirely forbidden, but if they are necessary they must be taken out with measure and prudence. It is important to know that they put the borrower in a position of weakness. The borrower is servant to the lender. The lender dominates the borrower and dictates his conduct in various areas.

Many people take out loans for the wrong reasons: impatience, covetousness, pride and lack of moderation. The one who wants to possess something rapidly is tempted to borrow money instead of saving it and waiting to be able to buy. He lacks patience and this impatience can be very costly not only in terms of interest but also in terms of freedom. If someone wants to obtain what he cannot afford, he becomes a potential client of the banks and the lending companies. Borrowing is a "solution" to avoid renouncing covetousness. Someone might desire to acquire goods that increase his social status or his image, but spending for the sake of prestige is expensive and irrational. Inspired by pride, this kind of spending is often neither necessary nor satisfying. A young couple would like to own a large dream house without first going through the small condominium of newlyweds. Their ambitions are excessive and will weigh a lot in their life.

**The lender dominates the borrower**

In a society where debt is presented as the path that everyone follows, it is important to remember that in many cases it is not necessary. There are solutions that make it possible to avoid taking out a loan. These alternative ways are linked to a paradigm of the world and an understanding of life renewed by God's wisdom. It is possible to summarize them in three principles:

- Start small
- Choose simplicity
- Save actively

Buying a car, furniture and housing are the three most frequent opportunities to take out a loan. Only the acquisition of housing can justify this, as cars and furniture quickly lose a great portion of their value. They will be worth nothing before the end of their repayment, making the borrower poorer than he was before. Only housing can conserve its value providing it was not bought overpriced.

**If we are not able to put money aside, we are not able to take out a loan anyway**

It is possible to use public transportation or a more modest personal vehicle until our savings allow us to consider something better. If we are not able to put money aside we are not able to take out a loan, anyway. Nothing can allow us to think that we will be able to pay it back. Acquisition of furniture can be also made progressively, according to our savings. It is possible to start small by getting some family furniture and then adding little by little. Taking out a loan for immediate consumable goods and services (holidays, clothing, electronics, leisure…) is a guarantee to becoming poorer. Debt stays while the goods are long gone. It is necessary to know how to say "no" to ourselves and renounce desires or pleasures that are too expensive for us.

Debt not only has a high price financially but also emotionally. Loans that are too large generate stress and anguish. When the burden of what is owed becomes too heavy, the borrowers lose their peace and find that they are at the mercy of their lenders. They realize that they can lose everything if they cannot honor their financial obligations. They are no longer masters of their possessions and other people dominate them. Because of loans taken out at the beginning of their adult life, many people have spent a significant part of their professional lives working for their banker instead of working for themselves. They have made themselves slaves through their debts.

**The borrowers lose their peace and find that they are at the mercy of their lenders**

# PLEASURES

*"He who loves pleasure will be a poor man; he who loves wine and oil will not be rich."*

Proverbs 21:17

It is possible to spend a good portion of our income on pleasures. Historically, the countries marked by the Reformation and its views of austerity have rapidly become more industrious and prosperous than the countries that stayed Catholic. The search for pleasures is not only costly in itself, but it also sets a path in life that does not lead to prosperity. Just as excessive drinking, excessive leisure and pleasures lead to a kind of intoxication. The perception of what is essential and the vision of life goals become blurry. The excess of entertainment generates a loss of clarity about the things to undertake and it maintains an atmosphere of laziness. It moves people away from work and the sense of responsibility. In this case, evenings are used for entertainment instead of studying, improving oneself, developing new skills, praying, serving for the community, preparing a new project or building family unity.

Society today encourages expenses geared toward leisure, entertainment and pleasure. Entertainment consumes not only money, but also the time of those who give themselves to it. The tendency to always desire more leisure time and fewer hours of work is very obvious in Western countries The value we place on professional activity diminishes while the importance we place on pleasures increases. This mentality will bring impoverishment which has started to be visible in many countries. Part of the new generation rejects a lifestyle of work without being aware that the comfort they enjoy is linked to it. Many do not realize that they are "surfing" the wave of social prosperity that their parents and grandparents acquired by their labor. On the other hand, in the global economy context, countries that give themselves to work and apply themselves to improving their production become influential actors.

A lifestyle[11] of recreational activities and luxurious food can swallow up significant resources and put a heavy strain on a budget without anyone being aware of it. Money regularly spent on these pleasures will be lacking when it is time to invest in a means of production or acquire a property that would raise the financial level of the family. A taste for luxury and immediate joy will nibble at the fruit of labor, like rodents established in the attic and unnoticed by its owner.

On the contrary, a simple lifestyle releases undreamt-of financial resources. Little by little, small amounts of money are preserved and saved in view of necessary investments for the family's future. Savings are made slowly, unobtrusively, regularly and in the long-term. They are the fruit of persevering and patient efforts sustained by the vision of a goal. For example, it is possible to pay cash for a small car by not buying a soda or coffee daily for ten years. Some families have never had the joy of owning their housing because their resources were used up throughout their lives to satisfy immediate pleasures.

[11] Occasional happy and extravagant feasts are part of an economically and emotionally balanced life. It is important to celebrate without restraint during special occasions (weddings, births, birthdays, feasts linked to faith…). But a lifestyle of constant pleasure is ruinous.

# PRESTIGE

*"Better is the one who is slighted but has a servant, than he who honors himself but lacks bread."*

Proverbs 12:9

Prestige is costly. Statistics show that in certain developing countries, small loans to women bring better results than credits to men. The reason is simple: because of their local culture, women are preoccupied with feeding their children, and men are more interested in advancing their social status. With their loans, women acquire means of production (for example a sewing machine), while men make expenditures (electronic devices or expensive clothing) that enhance their self-image. With their means of production women are able to feed their family and in time to pay back their loan. On the other hand, men do not generate new income and cannot pay back what was entrusted to them. Their frivolous expenditures have swallowed up everything without producing anything.

*"Better is the one who is slighted but has a servant, than he who honors himself but lacks bread."* Glamorous expenses indulge pride, but only for a season, then they show their vanity. We must prefer humble and productive solutions. Our society encourages us to acquire what is going to enhance our image in our own eyes or in the eyes of others. Nevertheless, our income is not linked to our self-image

**Our income is not linked to our self-image, but to our work and the work of our associates**

(with the exception of movie stars and TV personalities), but to our labor and the work of our associates. It is better to hire a good employee than to have a bronze nameplate and an office space in a prestigious business center.

Everything spent to project a "good image" of ourselves is costly and does not produce any income. It paralyzes and hinders the financial development of a company; at the worst, it puts its very existence in danger. Luxurious options considerably increase the price of a car or a house and can become an unbearable burden on the family budget. Simple and functional solutions often only cost a fraction of the price of those that aim to impress others. God loves humility and His ways are marked by humility. He gives success to the one who chooses humility.

**God gives success to the one who chooses humility**

## *SYNTHESIS: THE THREE PROSPERITY MINIMIZERS*

Debt, pleasures and prestige can limit our prosperity, particularly if they occupy a large place in our lives.

## *REFLECTION*

- Among these three minimizers, which ones could represent a danger to my prosperity?
- What correction should I bring to my lifestyle for that not to happen?

# Chapter 5

## RICH FOR WHAT?

It is interesting to see that most people who desire to have many possessions do not necessarily know why. Their goal is either to become rich or to escape poverty for good. All their thoughts and efforts are focused on that objective. Their reflection often stops there. But once the finish line is crossed, what will these possessions be used for?

This very question is a trap. In fact, when does one become rich? When can we consider that we have reached prosperity? Everyone answers this question in a different manner. God does not answer it.

Some say: "When I have the means, I will put this principle into practice; when I am rich, I will be able to give this or that." It is a wrong way of thinking. Actually, the person who gives when he has little will continue to give when he has much. The man who waits to become rich in order to be generous will probably not be liberal when he reaches wealth. Obedience to the Word and generosity are heart attitudes that do not depend on the amount of our possessions. There is no finish line after which everything will change. There is not a "before" or an "after" but a continuity and a progression. Our way of living is not influenced by our level of wealth but by our character. We simply do the same things with more or less financial means. The ways God teaches us at the beginning of the journey stay valid for the duration.

## HONORING GOD FIRST

*"Honor the LORD with your possessions, and with the firstfruits of all your increase; So your barns will be filled with plenty, and your vats will overflow with new wine."*

Proverbs 3:9-10

These words are addressed to the poor, to the rich and to the super rich. The destitute are not exempt from this commandment under the excuse that they are too poor. People who possess in abundance are not exempt either because their barns are already full. These exhortations and these promises are for all and they stay valid, whatever our situation. The poor will honor God with their goods according to the measure of their means and the rich will do so as well according to their resources.

Honoring God with one's possessions obviously involves the practice of tithes, offerings and alms. This is implied in Proverbs. These basic requirements constitute the foundations established before our first chapter. Because our aim is to reflect the wisdom of Proverbs we will not stop on these three important subjects. Nevertheless, they deserve to be treated in depth in another study.

Honoring God with our goods is not limited to contributing to His work in obedience to His Word. It does not only include supporting His servants, extending the Gospel and participating in the financial life of our congregation. We can be a sign in our family and society and give glory to God with all that we possess. We are called to testify of Him in the way we use our money. We have the possibility of managing our finances and running our business in a way that honors God. This way, people will know that He is much more important than gain. They will see that the Lord is before everything else and that we do not make our decisions based on money. They will perceive that we serve the God of righteousness because we deal fairly in business and use fair scales. Looking at the way we manage our business or our company, they will have the opportunity to question their conviction that money controls the world.

Honoring God with the firstfruits of all our income establishes a priority order: He is the first served. He comes first, before our needs and our projects. Giving the firstfruits of all we earn is a declaration of faith: "Lord God, You are first in my life, You come before everything else. You are the Best that I have on this earth; You are more important than me and my family. I trust You. You are good and I know that You take good care of me and mine."

For many, money only has an economic dimension. For some, finances are an economic and moral reality. For God money has a spiritual dimension first. The management of our goods manifests whom we adore. Money is a revealer. It reflects our spiritual state, it unveils our hearts. It exposes our deep passions. It expresses to whom we are attached. So, the use of our finances is a strong witnessing tool. In a world where money speaks loudly, let it say how much we love our God.

**In a world where money speaks loudly, let it say how much we love our God**

## HELPING THE POOR

*"He who has a generous eye will be blessed, for he gives of his bread to the poor."*

Proverbs 22:9

God has a generous eye upon the one who has a generous eye towards the poor. God blesses the one who blesses the underprivileged. Our attitude toward the destitute influences the relationship God maintains with us (and the one we have with Him.)

Riches are not evenly spread on the earth. In the same way, in a given country the distribution of goods varies enormously. There are rich and poor everywhere. An egalitarian society does not exist. The theories of the standardization of prosperity have never been able to be put into practice.

The rich need the poor and the poor need the rich. These roles can change along the course of life. God does not want to level out the differences, but He wants to use them to transform hearts. *"The rich and the poor have this in common, the Lord is the maker of them all[12]."*

**The rich need the poor and the poor need the rich**

[12] Proverbs 22:2

The rich man naturally thinks that he is wiser than the poor man[13]. His prosperity might make him proud. He imagines that he is superior to the one who has less than him. He considers that others have to learn from him and that he can give them lessons on how to succeed. The media confirm this idea because the public is interested in hearing what the wealthiest have to say.

The man living in abundance can also become hard of heart[14]. Unfortunately, to be rich as well as gentle and humble is rare. We often hear the saying: "He is hard in business." The man with a fortune runs the risk of becoming indifferent[15] because of his ties with money and his loss of contact with the needs of those who lack. God is looking for rich people who are kind, who reflect His character and are active agents of economic righteousness.

**God is looking for rich people who are gentle and humble**

God is very close to people who are destitute and takes their situation to heart. What a rich man does to the poor, he does the same to God. So, *he who has pity on the poor lends to the Lord.*[16] God considers that He is the beneficiary of a gift given to an impoverished person. He is eager to reimburse the giver. He identifies Himself with the destitute when someone

13 *"The rich man is wise in his own eyes, but the poor who has understanding searches him out."* Proverbs 28:11
14 *"The poor man uses entreaties, but the rich answers roughly."* Proverbs 18:23
15 *"He who gives to the poor will not lack, but he who hides his eyes will have many curses."* Proverbs 28:27
16 Proverbs 19:17

shows goodness to him, but also when someone hurts him. He who mocks the poor insults his Maker.[17] A person who harms the destitute offends the Lord. God has a very particular relationship with the poor; He protects them and defends them. He does not accept that wrong would be done to them. The one who mistreats them will always have to give account for it.

The man who has enough to give has a responsibility toward the one who lacks. His prosperity goes along with a mission of compassion. His duty is to help the poor. Delegating this task to the government is not acceptable. God entrusts him with goods so that His righteousness can be manifested and His love can be spread. The blessing of the Lord should never lead to an attitude of hardness, indifference or superiority. The poor need the rich materially as much as the rich need the poor spiritually. The direct transfer of riches from man to man without any delegation or system allows the poor as well as the rich to keep a tender, loving, grateful and righteous heart.

**His prosperity goes along with a mission of compassion**

[17] *"He who mocks the poor reproaches his Maker."* Proverbs 17:5

# ABOUT THE AUTHOR

Pierre Bezençon earned a master's degree in Theology in 1987. He has been in full-time pastoral ministry for more than 25 years.

With his wife he founded and leads "Foyers d'Amour" (Homes of Love), a Bible training center geared towards leaders and couples.

He and his wife are pastors of a congregation in Switzerland that they started in 2000. This community has become Messianic.

Since 2004 his teaching ministry has led him to the mission field in Africa to train and equip church leaders.

Pierre's favorite teaching themes are God's fatherhood, the extraordinary identity of Jesus, fellowship with the Holy Spirit, apostolic reformation, messianic reformation, the administration of the prophetic, edifying the church according to the divine model and all that concerns the life of couples and the role of the man.

Pierre Bezençon has written two books:

- On a pris mon Seigneur (They Have Taken My Lord)
- Mon Père et votre Père (My Father and Your Father)

He has recorded several teachings for men and for leaders as well as a Bible overview: "Bâtir sur le Roc" ("Building On the Rock").

Pierre and Laurence Bezençon live in French speaking Switzerland and in Kansas City, Missouri, where they join the life of the International House of Prayer (IHOPKC).

## PUBLICATIONS

The teachings of Pierre and Laurence Bezençon are designed to help you experience the love of God daily.

Laurence Bezençon has published two books:

- L'amour plus fort que l'abus (Love Stronger Than Abuse)
- Ton amour dans la souffrance (Your Love in Suffering)

She has created several audio series about the Holy Spirit healing broken hearts, specifically:

- Oints pour restaurer selon Esaïe 61 (Anointed to Restore, according to Isaiah 61)
- Sortir de la culture de l'abus (Getting Out of the Culture of Abuse)

Laurence Bezençon has taught on subjects concerning women and wives, like:

- Femmes de destinée et Femmes d'espérance (Women of Destiny and Women of Hope)
- Femmes de valeur et Développer l'amour pour son mari (Women of Value and Developing Love for Your Husband)

She also teaches on prayer, intimacy with God, Song of Songs and other similar subjects.

To contact Homes of Love
www.homes-of-love.com
Email: homesoflovepublishers@gmail.com

For a complete list of available titles in French: www.labible.ch.